B
BIRDS

AN URBAN BIRDWATCHING LOGBOOK
ILLUSTRATIONS BY CHRISTINE BERRIE

LAURENCE KING PUBLISHING

[01] **AFRICAN PARADISE FLYCATCHER**
[02] **AMERICAN GOLDFINCH**
[03] **AMERICAN KESTREL**
[04] **AMERICAN ROBIN**
[05] **BARN OWL**
[06] **BLUE JAY**
[07] **BLUE TIT**
[08] **BOHEMIAN WAXWING**
[09] **BROWN PELICAN**

[10] **CAMPO FLICKER**
[11] **CANADA GOOSE**
[12] **CAROLINA CHICKADEE**
[13] **CAROLINA WREN**
[14] **CHINESE POND HERON**
[15] **COMMON GRACKLE**
[16] **DARK-EYED JUNCO**
[17] **EASTERN BLUEBIRD**
[18] **EUROPEAN BEE-EATER**

[19] **EUROPEAN ROBIN**
[20] **EUROPEAN STARLING**
[21] **GOLDEN ORIOLE**
[22] **GREAT BLUE HERON**
[23] **GREAT HORNED OWL**
[24] **HAMERKOP**
[25] **HOOPOE**
[26] **HOUSE SPARROW**
[27] **LAUGHING KOOKABURRA**

[26]
[27]
[29]
[31]
[28]
[30]
[32]
[33]
[34]
[35]
[39]
[36]
[37]
[38]
[41]
[45]
[42]
[44]
[43]
[40]
[46]
[49]
[47]
[48]
[50]

[28] **MAGNIFICENT FRIGATEBIRD**
[29] **MAGPIE**
[30] **MALLARD**
[31] **MONK PARAKEET**
[32] **MOURNING DOVE**
[33] **NORTHERN CARDINAL**
[34] **NORTHERN MOCKINGBIRD**
[35] **ORIENTAL WHITE-EYE**
[36] **PEREGRINE FALCON**

[37] **PIED (WHITE) WAGTAIL**
[38] **PURPLE MARTIN**
[39] **RAINBOW LORIKEET**
[40] **RED-HEADED WOODPECKER**
[41] **RED-WHISKERED BULBUL**
[42] **RED-WINGED BLACKBIRD**
[43] **RUBY-THROATED HUMMINGBIRD**
[44] **SERIN**
[45] **SULPHUR-CRESTED COCKATOO**

[46] **SUPERB FAIRYWREN**
[47] **SUPERB STARLING**
[48] **TURKEY VULTURE**
[49] **WHITE-BREASTED KINGFISHER**
[50] **WHITE-BREASTED NUTHATCH**

[01]

AFRICAN PARADISE FLYCATCHER
Terpsiphone viridis

Small, with black crest, blue eye-ring, chestnut upperparts and, in the male, extravagant tail streamers. Darts out from perch to capture insects in flight. Builds tiny cup-shaped nest, from which male's long tail dangles while sitting.

LENGTH	11–13¾ in	28–35 cm
WINGSPAN	±9¾ in	25 cm
WEIGHT	up to ½ oz	12–14 g

DISTRIBUTION Sub-Saharan Africa and southern Arabian Peninsula; savannah woodland and open forest, including parks and backyards.

TIME & DATE

LOCATION

BEHAVIOR

FEMALE-MALE

WEATHER

OTHER

[02]

AMERICAN GOLDFINCH

Spinus tristis

Male small and bright lemon yellow; female duller. Dangles from plants while extracting seeds with conical bill. Forms large flocks outside breeding season, migrating short distances. Common in towns, where it benefits from backyard feeders.

LENGTH	$4\frac{1}{4}$–$5\frac{1}{2}$ in	11–14 cm	DISTRIBUTION Across North America
WINGSPAN	$7\frac{1}{2}$–$8\frac{3}{4}$ in	19–22 cm	from coast to coast; open habitats,
WEIGHT	$\frac{1}{2}$–$\frac{3}{4}$ oz	11–20 g	including residential areas.

TIME & DATE

LOCATION

BEHAVIOR

FEMALE-MALE

WEATHER

OTHER

[03]

AMERICAN KESTREL

Falco sparverius

Smallest American raptor, with blue-gray and rufous plumage. Feeds on grasshoppers, lizards, and rodents. Hunts from perch or by hovering in mid-air, swooping to snatch prey from ground. A beginner's bird in falconry.

LENGTH	$8\frac{3}{4}$–$12\frac{1}{4}$ in	22–31 cm	
WINGSPAN	20–24 in	51–61 cm	
WEIGHT	$2\frac{3}{4}$–$5\frac{3}{4}$ oz	80–165 g	

DISTRIBUTION North and South America, from Alaska to Patagonia; prefers open habitats, including suburban areas.

TIME & DATE

LOCATION

BEHAVIOR

FEMALE-MALE

WEATHER

OTHER

[04]

AMERICAN ROBIN
Turdus migratorius

Medium-sized thrush. Named for red-orange breast, which resembles that of European robin. Very common and widespread. Feeds on insects, fruit, and berries, often foraging on lawns. Known for blue eggs and complex song. Northern populations migrate south in winter.

LENGTH	9–11 in	23–28 cm	DISTRIBUTION Across North America;
WINGSPAN	12–16 in	31–41 cm	most habitats, including
WEIGHT	2½–3¼ oz	72–94 g	residential areas.

TIME & DATE

LOCATION

BEHAVIOR

FEMALE-MALE

WEATHER

OTHER

[05]

BARN OWL
Tyto alba

Pure white underparts and heart-shaped face. Hunts rodents at dusk or
after dark using powerful hearing and agile, silent flight. Often nests
in old buildings. Spectral appearance and eerie, hissing calls have
inspired ghost stories.

LENGTH $13-15\frac{1}{4}$ in   33–39 cm
WINGSPAN $31\frac{1}{2}-37\frac{1}{2}$ in   80–95 cm
WEIGHT $8\frac{3}{4}-17\frac{1}{2}$ oz   250–500 g

DISTRIBUTION All continents except
Antarctica; open country, often
around farms.

TIME & DATE

LOCATION

BEHAVIOR

FEMALE-MALE

WEATHER

OTHER

[06]

BLUE JAY

Cyanocitta cristata

Blue and white with blue crest and black collar. Readily visits garden feeders. Intelligent, like other members of crow family: mimics the calls of raptors, collects shiny objects and may bury food to collect later.

LENGTH	8¾–12 in	22–30 cm
WINGSPAN	13½–17 in	34–43 cm
WEIGHT	2½–3½ oz	70–100 g

DISTRIBUTION North America, mostly east of the Rockies; woodland and residential areas.

TIME & DATE

LOCATION

BEHAVIOR

FEMALE-MALE

WEATHER

OTHER

[07]

BLUE TIT

Cyanistes caeruleus

Small, colorful, and acrobatic. Often feeds upside down and commonly visits backyard bird feeders. Nests in tree holes and takes readily to nest boxes. One pair may collect 10,000 caterpillars for their nestlings in three weeks.

LENGTH	4½ in	11.5 cm	DISTRIBUTION Common across Europe,
WINGSPAN	7 in	18 cm	including Britain; woodland, parks,
WEIGHT	½ oz	11 g	and backyards.

TIME & DATE

LOCATION

BEHAVIOR

FEMALE-MALE

WEATHER

OTHER

[08]

BOHEMIAN WAXWING
Bombycilla garrulus

Starling-sized, with crest. Breeds in northern forests; migrates south
in winter, sometimes visiting the UK. Gets its name from the red,
wax-like tips to its secondary wing feathers. Flocks to ornamental
berry bushes in towns.

LENGTH	7½–9 in	19–23 cm	DISTRIBUTION Northern Eurasia and
WINGSPAN	12½–13¾ in	32–35 cm	North America; irregular winter
WEIGHT	1½–2½ oz	45–70 g	visitor to the UK.

TIME & DATE

LOCATION

BEHAVIOR

FEMALE-MALE

WEATHER

OTHER

[09]

BROWN PELICAN
Pelecanus occidentalis

Very large seabird with huge bill and broad wings. Catches fish by
diving headfirst into sea from the air. Stores catch in an expandable
pouch of skin below its bill. Breed in colonies on islands and
mangroves.

LENGTH	42–54 in	106–137 cm	DISTRIBUTION Atlantic and Pacific
WINGSPAN	6–8¼ ft	1.83–2.5 m	coasts of North America, south
WEIGHT	6–12 lb	2.75–5.5 kg	to northern South America and
			Caribbean; common on coasts.

TIME & DATE

LOCATION

BEHAVIOR

FEMALE-MALE

WEATHER

OTHER

[10]

CAMPO FLICKER
Colaptes campestris

Ground-feeding woodpecker with black, yellow, and red face and head. Often feeds in small groups, hopping about in search of termites, ants, and beetles. May hammer holes in termite mounds. Nests in tree holes.

LENGTH   11–12¼ in   28–31 cm
WINGSPAN   16½–20 in   42–51 cm
WEIGHT   5–6¾ oz   145–192 g

DISTRIBUTION Eastern South America, from central Brazil to central Argentina; open country, savanna, and pampas.

TIME & DATE

LOCATION

BEHAVIOR

FEMALE-MALE

WEATHER

OTHER

[11]

CANADA GOOSE
Branta canadensis

Large, long-necked goose with black and white head. Races vary in size. Feeds on grass and grain. Has colonized residential areas across its range. Feral populations thrive in parks and towns across Europe. Flocks migrate in V formation.

LENGTH	30–43 in	75–110 cm
WINGSPAN	50–73 in	127–185 cm
WEIGHT	$5\frac{3}{4}$–$14\frac{1}{4}$ lb	2.6–6.5 kg

DISTRIBUTION Widespread across North America; introduced to Europe and New Zealand.

TIME & DATE

LOCATION

BEHAVIOR

FEMALE-MALE

WEATHER

OTHER

CAROLINA CHICKADEE

Poecile carolinensis

Small, with black and white head. Feeds acrobatically on insects in woodland trees. Diet changes to seeds and berries in winter, when it regularly visits bird feeders. Nests in tree holes. Named for "chick-a-dee, dee, dee" call.

LENGTH	$4\frac{1}{2}$–5 in	11.5–13 cm
WINGSPAN	$7\frac{1}{2}$–$8\frac{1}{2}$ in	19–21.5 cm
WEIGHT	$\frac{1}{4}$–$\frac{1}{2}$ oz	9–12 g

DISTRIBUTION Eastern USA; mixed woodland, parks, and backyards.

TIME & DATE

LOCATION

BEHAVIOR

FEMALE-MALE

WEATHER

OTHER

[13]

CAROLINA WREN

Thryothorus ludovicianus

Small, but large for a wren, with perky tail and bold eyebrow. Sticks
to cover, where more often heard than seen. Song contains over
30 separate phrases. Forages for invertebrates at ground level.
State bird of South Carolina.

LENGTH	$4\frac{3}{4}$–$5\frac{1}{2}$ in	12–14 cm	
WINGSPAN	$11\frac{1}{2}$ in	29 cm	
WEIGHT	$\frac{1}{2}$–$\frac{3}{4}$ oz	18–23 g	

DISTRIBUTION Eastern USA south to
northeast Mexico; woodland, swamps,
and overgrown habitats, including
in urban areas.

TIME & DATE

LOCATION

BEHAVIOR

FEMALE-MALE

WEATHER

OTHER

[14]

CHINESE POND HERON

Ardeola bacchus

Small, compact heron. Inconspicuous when perched but reveals striking white wings in flight. Feeds at the water's edge, alone or in small, scattered groups. Snatches fish, frogs, and invertebrates with dagger bill.

LENGTH $18\frac{1}{2}$ in   47 cm
WINGSPAN $9\frac{3}{4}$–11 in   75–90 in
WEIGHT   13 oz   370 g

DISTRIBUTION China and eastern Asia, migrating south in winter; ponds, ditches, and freshwater wetlands, including in built-up areas.

TIME & DATE

LOCATION

BEHAVIOR

FEMALE-MALE

WEATHER

OTHER

[15]

COMMON GRACKLE
Quiscalus quiscula

Iridescent black plumage, yellowish eyes, and strong bill. Omnivorous: feeds on the ground, often stealing food from other birds. Very numerous in some built-up areas, often scavenging from outdoor eating sites. Breeds in colonies. Name comes from grating song.

LENGTH	11–13½ in	28–34 cm	
WINGSPAN	14–18 in	36–46 cm	
WEIGHT	2½–5 oz	74–142 g	

DISTRIBUTION Eastern North America—range has expanded west with forest clearance; open, semi-open, and built-up areas.

TIME & DATE

LOCATION

BEHAVIOR

FEMALE-MALE

WEATHER

OTHER

[16]

DARK-EYED JUNCO

Junco hyemalis

Sparrow-sized, with pale bill, gray head, and striking white outer tail feathers. Lives in forests and forages on the ground for insects and seeds. Northern populations may migrate south in winter. Flocks to spilt seed below feeders.

LENGTH	5–7 in	13–17.5 cm	DISTRIBUTION Across North America, including Alaska and Arctic Canada; coniferous and mixed forest.
WINGSPAN	7–9¾ in	18–25 cm	
WEIGHT	¾–1 oz	18–30 g	

TIME & DATE

LOCATION

BEHAVIOR

FEMALE-MALE

WEATHER

OTHER

[17]

EASTERN BLUEBIRD
Sialia sialias

Small and upright. Male vivid blue above and brick-red below; female less colorful. Perches on wires and posts, fluttering down to capture insects on ground. Nests in tree holes and takes readily to nest boxes. Will visit feeders for mealworms.

LENGTH	$6\frac{1}{4}$–$8\frac{1}{4}$ in	16–21 cm	
WINGSPAN	$9\frac{3}{4}$–$12\frac{1}{2}$ in	25–32 cm	
WEIGHT	1–$1\frac{1}{4}$ oz	27–34 g	

DISTRIBUTION Eastern North America; woodland edges and open areas, including backyards.

TIME & DATE

LOCATION

BEHAVIOR

FEMALE-MALE

WEATHER

OTHER

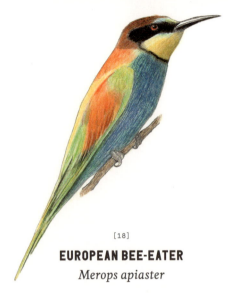

[18]

EUROPEAN BEE-EATER

Merops apiaster

Dazzling plumage, pointed tail, and agile, floating flight. Hunts from
perch, capturing bees and other insects in mid-air. Can eat 250 bees
a day. Colonies nest in sand banks, each pair digging its own tunnel.

LENGTH	10–11½ in	27–29 cm	
WINGSPAN	14–15¾ in	36–40 cm	
WEIGHT	1½–2¾ oz	44–78 g	

DISTRIBUTION Breeds in Mediterranean
Europe and east/central Asia;
migrates in winter to Africa and
southern Asia; open country.

TIME & DATE

LOCATION

BEHAVIOR

FEMALE-MALE

WEATHER

OTHER

[19]

EUROPEAN ROBIN

Erithacus rubecula

Bright orange breast, bold demeanor and delicate song. Often feeds around gardeners, taking insects from soil. Association with Christmas stems from Victorian postmen, who wore red and were nicknamed "Robin." Belongs to flycatcher family; unrelated to American robin.

LENGTH	5–5½ in	12.5–14 cm	DISTRIBUTION Europe, Western Asia,
WINGSPAN	8–8¾ in	20–22 cm	and North Africa; very common
WEIGHT	½–¾ oz	16–22 g	in the UK.

TIME & DATE

LOCATION

BEHAVIOR

FEMALE-MALE

WEATHER

OTHER

[20]

EUROPEAN STARLING

Sturnus vulgaris

Iridescent black plumage and sharp bill. Common in towns. Nests in holes and mimics other birds in its inventive song. Highly sociable; outside breeding season may roost in huge flocks that perform spectacular aerial displays. Destructive invader where introduced.

LENGTH	7½–9 in	19–23 cm	
WINGSPAN	12¼–17¼ in	31–44 cm	
WEIGHT	2–3½ oz	58–101 g	

DISTRIBUTION Native to Europe and western Asia; introduced to North and South America, Australia; open habitats and built-up areas.

TIME & DATE

LOCATION

BEHAVIOR

FEMALE-MALE

WEATHER

OTHER

[21]

GOLDEN ORIOLE

Oriolus oriolus

Thrush-sized, fruit-eating songbird with fluting call. Male brilliant
yellow and black; female leaf green. Shy; usually glimpsed flitting
between trees. Summer visitor from Africa. "Oriole" derives from Latin
aureolas, meaning "golden."

LENGTH $8\frac{1}{2}$–$9\frac{3}{4}$ in   22–25 cm
WINGSPAN   18 in   46 cm
WEIGHT $2\frac{1}{4}$–$2\frac{3}{4}$ oz   60–80 g

DISTRIBUTION Breeds from southern and
central Europe to Central Asia;
winters in sub-Saharan Africa; open
woodland, orchards, and plantations.

TIME & DATE

LOCATION

BEHAVIOR

FEMALE-MALE

WEATHER

OTHER

[22]

GREAT BLUE HERON

Ardea herodias

Very tall, with long neck and long legs. Always found near water.
Feeds on fish, frogs, small mammals, and other mostly aquatic prey,
seizing victim in dagger-like bill. Colonies breed in treetops,
often on islands.

LENGTH	6¼–8¼ in	91–137 cm
WINGSPAN	66–79 in	167–201 cm
WEIGHT	4–8 lb	1.8–3.6 kg

DISTRIBUTION Across North America, north to Alaska; aquatic habitats inland and on coast, including built-up areas where fish thrive.

TIME & DATE

LOCATION

BEHAVIOR

FEMALE-MALE

WEATHER

OTHER

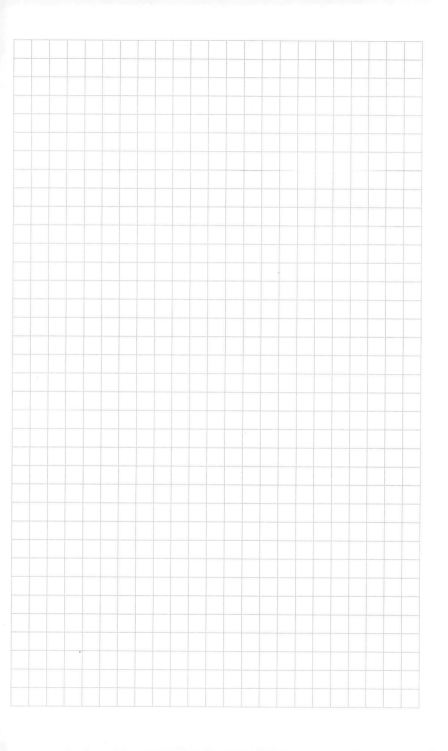

[23]

GREAT HORNED OWL
Bubo virginianus

Big and fierce-looking, with cryptic plumage and prominent ear tufts. Commonest large owl in the Americas. Hunts by night for variety of prey, from insects to jackrabbits. Grip of talons five times stronger than human hand.

LENGTH	7–25 in	43–64 cm
WINGSPAN	3–5 ft	91–153 cm
WEIGHT	2½–5½ lb	1.2–2.5 kg

DISTRIBUTION North, Central, and South America, from Alaskan sub-Arctic to Argentinian pampas; most habitats, including residential areas.

TIME & DATE 9:02 PM Tus 9-8-20

LOCATION back yard

BEHAVIOR

FEMALE-MALE

WEATHER

OTHER

[24]

HAMERKOP

Scopus umbretta

Brown, heron-like water bird in family of its own. Crested head has
hammer-like shape, hence Afrikaans name. Enormous domed nest is often
used by other birds, including geese and owls. Feared as evil omen
in some African cultures.

LENGTH	22 in	56 cm
WINGSPAN	$35\frac{1}{2}$–37 in	44–48 cm
WEIGHT	$14\frac{1}{2}$–15 oz	46–89 g

DISTRIBUTION Sub-Saharan Africa and
southern Arabian Peninsula; common
around most wetlands and water
bodies, including in built-up areas.

TIME & DATE

LOCATION

BEHAVIOR

FEMALE-MALE

WEATHER

OTHER

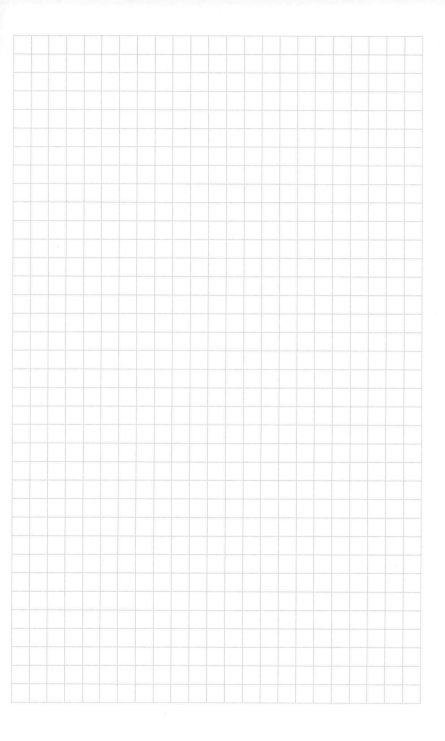

[25]

HOOPOE

Upupa epops

Long crest, striking colors, and thin, curved bill. In floppy, undulating flight resembles large moth. Nests in tree holes and probes for food in ground, often lawns. Named for repetitive "hoop hoop hoop" call, given with crest fanned.

LENGTH $9\frac{3}{4}$–$12\frac{1}{2}$ in   25–32 cm
WINGSPAN $17\frac{1}{4}$–19 in   44–48 cm
WEIGHT $1\frac{1}{2}$–$3\frac{1}{4}$ oz   46–89 g

DISTRIBUTION Southern Europe, Asia, north and sub-Saharan Africa; variety of open habitats, including parks and farmland.

TIME & DATE

LOCATION

BEHAVIOR

FEMALE-MALE

WEATHER

OTHER

[26]

HOUSE SPARROW
Passer domesticus

Small and compact. Thrives around towns and human habitation. Uses
thick bill to feed on seed and spilled grain. Originally from Middle
East, but has since spread (via ships) to every continent
except Antarctica.

LENGTH	$6\frac{1}{4}$ in	16 cm
WINGSPAN	$8\frac{1}{4}$–$9\frac{3}{4}$ in	21–25 cm
WEIGHT	$\frac{3}{4}$–1 oz	24–30 g

DISTRIBUTION The most widespread bird
in the world—Europe, Asia, Africa,
Americas, Australasia; towns and
farmland.

TIME & DATE

LOCATION

BEHAVIOR

FEMALE-MALE

WEATHER

OTHER

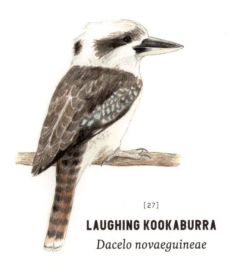

[27]

LAUGHING KOOKABURRA
Dacelo novaeguineae

Crow-sized kingfisher with powerful bill. Named for its ear-splitting territorial call, given at dawn and dusk, with several individuals often joining a competitive chorus. Common in suburbia. Captures reptiles, mice, and other small prey from the ground.

LENGTH	15–17 in	39–42 cm	
WINGSPAN	22–25 in	56–66 cm	
WEIGHT	11–17 oz	310–480 g	

DISTRIBUTION Native to eastern Australia and introduced to southwest; also New Guinea; open woodland, parks, and suburbia.

TIME & DATE

LOCATION

BEHAVIOUR

FEMALE-MALE

WEATHER

OTHER

[28]

MAGNIFICENT FRIGATEBIRD

Fregata magnificens

Large, black seabird with very long wings and long forked tail. So lightweight, its plumage weighs more than its skeleton. Male inflates red throat sac during breeding display. Snatches fish from the ocean surface and pirates food from other birds.

LENGTH	35–45 in	89–114 cm
WINGSPAN	85–96 in	217–244 cm
WEIGHT	2½–3½ lb	1.1–1.6 kg

DISTRIBUTION Tropical Atlantic and Pacific coasts of Americas, from Florida to Brazil; commonly seen soaring over coastal cities.

TIME & DATE

LOCATION

BEHAVIOR

FEMALE-MALE

WEATHER

OTHER

MAGPIE

Pica pica

Black-and-white plumage and long tail. Noisy, rattling call. Broad
diet includes eggs and nestlings. Belongs to crow family. Renowned
for curiosity and intelligence: can recognize itself in mirror. Some
scientists class American (black-billed) as a separate species.

LENGTH	$17\frac{1}{4}$–18 in	44–46 cm	DISTRIBUTION Europe, Asia, North
WINGSPAN	$20\frac{1}{2}$–$24\frac{1}{2}$ in	52–62 cm	America; common in towns and
WEIGHT	180–270 g	180–270 g	most open habitats.

TIME & DATE

LOCATION

BEHAVIOR

FEMALE-MALE

WEATHER

OTHER

[30]

MALLARD

Anas platyrhynchos

Large, ubiquitous duck. Colorful male has dark green head and yellow bill; female mottled brown. A dabbler: upends to feed on tiny aquatic plants and animals. Ancestor of most domestic ducks worldwide. Native across northern hemisphere; introduced elsewhere.

LENGTH	20–26 in	50–65 cm
WINGSPAN	32–39 in	81–98 cm
WEIGHT	1½–3½ lb	0.7–1.6 kg

DISTRIBUTION Europe, Asia, North America, Australia, New Zealand; abundant in most aquatic habitats, including town ponds and lakes.

TIME & DATE

LOCATION

BEHAVIOR

FEMALE-MALE

WEATHER

OTHER

[31]

MONK PARAKEET

Myiopsitta monachus

Starling-sized parrot, with long tail. Largely green and yellow,
revealing blue wings in flight. The only parrot that builds a stick
nest. Breeds colonially in treetops. Intelligent and sociable;
popular as a pet.

LENGTH	11½ in	29 cm	DISTRIBUTION Sub-tropical South
WINGSPAN	19 in	48 cm	America, notably Argentina and
WEIGHT	3½ oz	100 g	Brazil; thrives in cities; feral
			populations in Florida and Spain.

TIME & DATE

LOCATION

BEHAVIOR

FEMALE-MALE

WEATHER

OTHER

[32]

MOURNING DOVE
Zenaida macroura

Slender, gray/brown dove with purple neck patches. Abundant in most habitats, including urban areas. Prolific breeder, raising up to six broods per year. Hunters shoot more than 20 million annually.

LENGTH	12¼ in	31 cm	
WINGSPAN	17–19 in	43–48 cm	
WEIGHT	4–6 oz	112–170 g	

DISTRIBUTION North America, from southern Canada to Mexico; most habitats, except forest.

TIME & DATE

LOCATION

BEHAVIOR

FEMALE-MALE

WEATHER

OTHER

[33]

NORTHERN CARDINAL

Cardinalis cardinalis

Thick bill and perky crest. Male mostly bright red; female browner.
Feeds on seeds, berries, and insects, often visiting feeders. Males
chase away territorial rivals. Once prized as a cage bird for its
bright colors and lively song.

LENGTH $8\frac{1}{4}$–$9\frac{1}{4}$ in   21–23.5 cm   DISTRIBUTION North America east of
WINGSPAN $9\frac{3}{4}$–$12\frac{1}{4}$ in   25–31 cm   the Rockies, from southern Canada
WEIGHT $1\frac{1}{4}$–$2\frac{1}{4}$ oz   33.6–65 g   to Mexico.

TIME & DATE

LOCATION

BEHAVIOR

FEMALE-MALE

WEATHER

OTHER

[34]

NORTHERN MOCKINGBIRD
Mimus polyglottos

Medium-sized gray and white songbird with long legs and tail. Common in parks and backyards, often feeding on lawns. Loud song includes phrases from other birds. Defends nest fiercely. Official bird of five US states.

LENGTH	8–11 in	20.5–28 cm	
WINGSPAN	12¼–15 in	31–38 cm	
WEIGHT	1½–2 oz	40–58 g	

DISTRIBUTION North America, from southern Canada to Mexico and Caribbean; open habitats, including residential areas.

TIME & DATE

LOCATION

BEHAVIOR

FEMALE-MALE

WEATHER

OTHER

[35]

ORIENTAL WHITE-EYE
Zosterops palpebrosus

Small and delicate-looking; white, green, and yellow, with white ring around eye. Small groups forage in trees and bushes for nectar and small insects, calling constantly. Bathes in dew that gathers on leaves.

LENGTH	$3\frac{3}{4}$–$4\frac{1}{4}$ in	9.6–11 cm
WINGSPAN	±7 in	18 cm
WEIGHT	up to $\frac{1}{2}$ oz	5.6–11 g

DISTRIBUTION South and southeast Asia, from Pakistan to Indonesia; woodland, scrub, parks, and backyards.

TIME & DATE

LOCATION

BEHAVIOR

FEMALE-MALE

WEATHER

OTHER

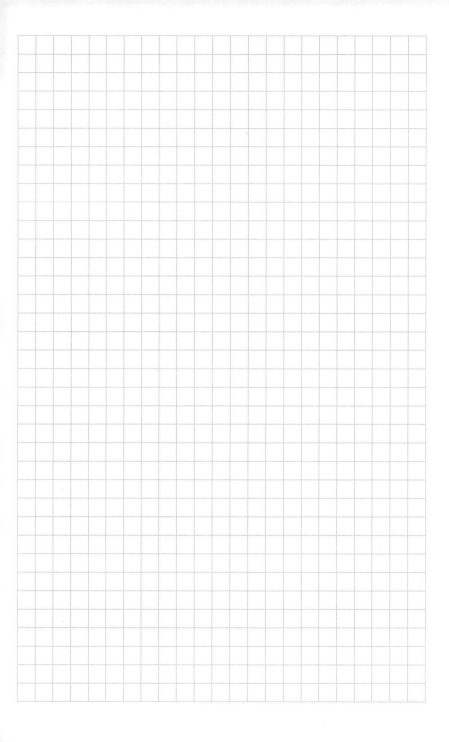

[36]

PEREGRINE FALCON
Falco peregrinus

Dashing raptor with black cap and anchor shape in flight. Fastest known
bird, exceeding 155 mph (250 kph) in aerial pursuit of other birds.
Nests on cliffs, especially along coasts. Adapts to urban environments,
breeding on tall buildings. Wanders widely outside breeding season.

LENGTH	14–19 in	36–49 cm	DISTRIBUTION Every continent except
WINGSPAN	39–43 in	100–110 cm	Antarctica; hunts over most
WEIGHT	19–57 oz	530–1,600 g	habitats and now breeds in New
			York, London, and other cities.

TIME & DATE	LOCATION

BEHAVIOR	FEMALE-MALE

WEATHER	OTHER

[37]

PIED (WHITE) WAGTAIL
Motacilla alba

Small, with black-and-white plumage. Constant wagging of long tail is
thought to signal vigilance to predators. Forages energetically on
ground for insects, usually near water, and often on sidewalks and in
car parks. May gather for warmth in large downtown winter roosts.

LENGTH	7 in	18 cm	DISTRIBUTION Europe and Asia;
WINGSPAN	9¾–12 in	25–30 cm	widespread, including in towns.
WEIGHT	1 oz	25 g	

TIME & DATE

LOCATION

BEHAVIOR

FEMALE-MALE

WEATHER

OTHER

[38]

PURPLE MARTIN

Progne subis

Large swallow with short tail and (in male) glossy blue-black plumage.
Eats insects and migrates south in winter. Breeds around human
habitation, but is losing out to invasive house sparrows and European
starlings. Dependent on nest boxes in many areas.

LENGTH	7–8 in	18–21 cm	DISTRIBUTION Breeds across North
WINGSPAN	15–16 in	39–42 cm	America and winters in tropical
WEIGHT	1½–2 oz	45–60 g	South America; open habitats,
			usually around people.

TIME & DATE

LOCATION

BEHAVIOR

FEMALE-MALE

WEATHER

OTHER

[39]

RAINBOW LORIKEET

Trichoglossus moluccanus

Dove-sized parrot, with vivid colors and long tail. Feeds acrobatically in trees, using special brush-like tongue to extract nectar and pollen. Visits bird tables for fruit and seeds. May become tame enough to feed by hand.

LENGTH	9¾–11¾ in	25–30 cm
WINGSPAN	17¾ in	45 cm
WEIGHT	2¾–5½ oz	75–157 g

DISTRIBUTION Australia's eastern seaboard, from northern Queensland to Tasmania; rainforest and coastal bush, common in suburbia.

TIME & DATE

LOCATION

BEHAVIOR

FEMALE-MALE

WEATHER

OTHER

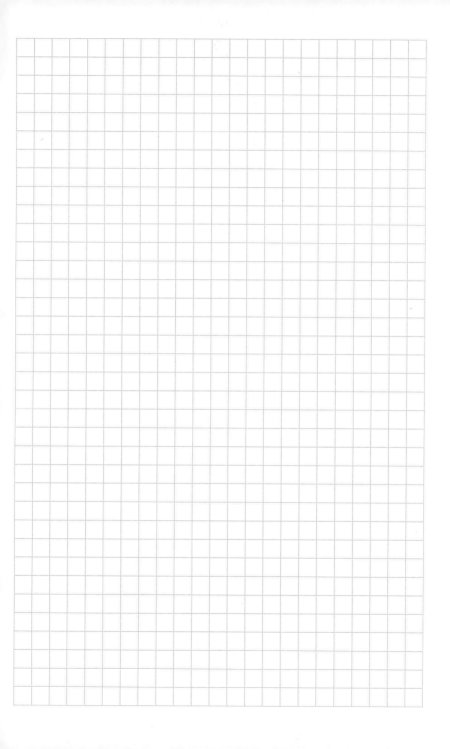

[40]

RED-HEADED WOODPECKER

Melanerpes erythrocephalus

Striking black-and-white body set off by bright red head and neck.
Omnivorous: feeds on trees like other woodpeckers, but also catches
insects in flight. Excavates nest hole in dead wood. Declining in
areas where old trees are removed.

LENGTH	7½–9¾ in	19–25 cm
WINGSPAN	16¾ in	42.5 cm
WEIGHT	2–3½ oz	56–97 g

DISTRIBUTION Eastern North America;
northern populations migrate
south in winter; open woodland
habitats, parks, and backyards.

TIME & DATE

LOCATION

BEHAVIOR

FEMALE-MALE

WEATHER

OTHER

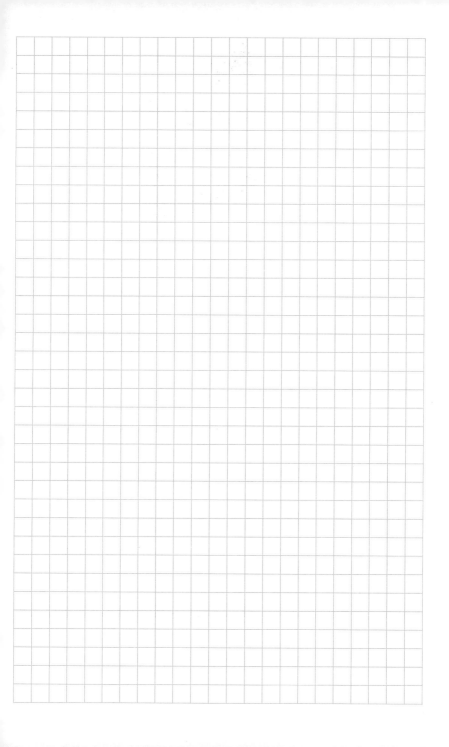

[41]

RED-WHISKERED BULBUL

Pycnonotus jocosus

Thrush-sized, with pointed black crest and red face patch. Eats fruits,
nectar, and insects. Common in parks and backyards, drawing attention
with loud three-note call. Unwelcome non-native alien in some tropical
regions around the world, including Australia and Hawaii.

LENGTH	8-8¾ in	20-22 cm
WINGSPAN	9¾-11 in	25-28 cm
WEIGHT	¾-1½ oz	23-42 g

DISTRIBUTION Tropical south and
southeast Asia; introduced to
many tropical islands; lightly
wooded areas, including suburbia.

TIME & DATE

LOCATION

BEHAVIOR

FEMALE-MALE

WEATHER

OTHER

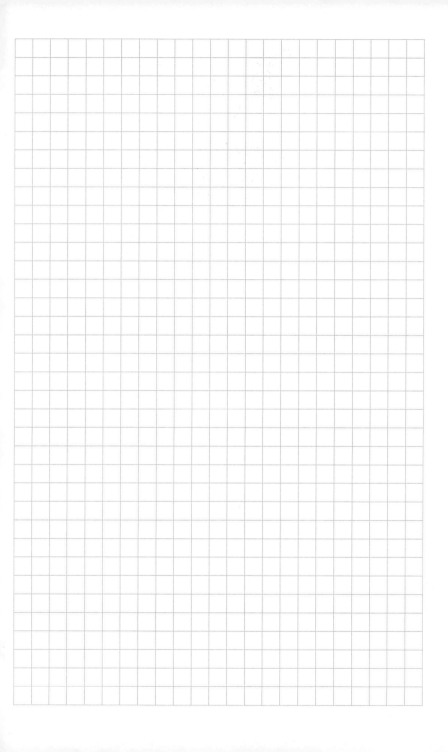

[42]

RED-WINGED BLACKBIRD

Agelaius phoeniceus

Starling-sized. Male black with red epaulettes; smaller female brown. The most numerous bird in North America: loose flocks may number over one million and can cause serious agricultural damage. Northern populations migrate south in winter. Omnivorous; visits bird feeders.

LENGTH	6¾–9½ in	17–24 cm
WINGSPAN	12¼–15¾ in	31–40 cm
WEIGHT	1–3 oz	29–82 g

DISTRIBUTION North and Central America, breeding from Alaska to Costa Rica; open areas, including marshes, wetlands, and meadows.

TIME & DATE

LOCATION

BEHAVIOR

FEMALE-MALE

WEATHER

OTHER

[43]

RUBY-THROATED HUMMINGBIRD
Archilochus colubris

Tiny, with needle-like bill and metallic green upperparts. Only male
has red throat. Sips nectar from flowers while hovering. Visits
backyard feeders. Beats wings at up to 75 times per second. Migrates
900 miles (1,450 km) non-stop across Gulf of Mexico.

LENGTH	$2\frac{3}{4}$–$3\frac{1}{2}$ in	7–9 cm	
WINGSPAN	$3\frac{1}{4}$–$4\frac{1}{4}$ in	8–11 cm	
WEIGHT	up to $\frac{1}{4}$ oz	2–6 g	

DISTRIBUTION Breeds in eastern
North America, southern Canada
to Mexico; winters in Central
America; woods, parks, backyards.

TIME & DATE

LOCATION

BEHAVIOR

FEMALE-MALE

WEATHER

OTHER

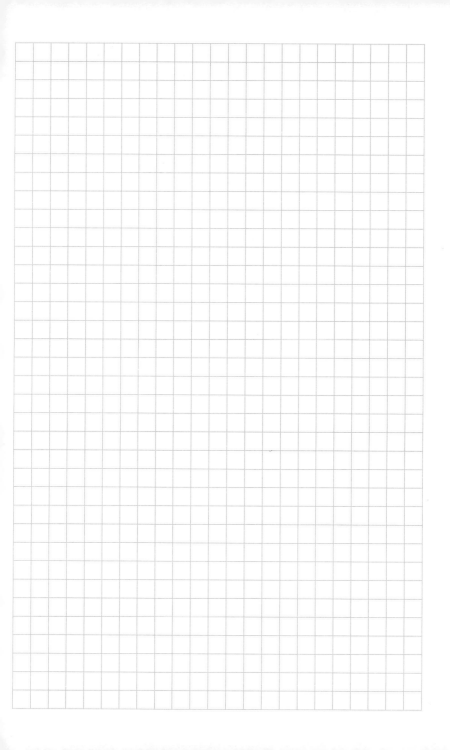

[44]

SERIN

Serinus serinus

Smallest European finch, closely related to canary. Male yellow; female browner. Stubby bill and forked tail. Feeds on seeds, buds and flowers, foraging near ground. Buzzing trill from treetop is a common spring sound around the Mediterranean.

LENGTH	$4\frac{1}{4}$–$4\frac{3}{4}$ in	11–12 cm	DISTRIBUTION South and central
WINGSPAN	$8\frac{1}{4}$–$9\frac{1}{4}$ in	21–23.7 cm	Europe, east to Russia; winters
WEIGHT	$\frac{1}{4}$–$\frac{1}{2}$ oz	8.5–14 g	in North Africa; woodland edges,
			suburbia, parks, and backyards.

TIME & DATE

LOCATION

BEHAVIOR

FEMALE-MALE

WEATHER

OTHER

[45]

SULPHUR-CRESTED COCKATOO
Cacatua galerita

Large white parrot with powerful bill and jaunty yellow crest. Raucous
call. Feeds on berries, nuts, and seeds, using tongue and toes to
manipulate food. May live over 70 years in captivity. Very intelligent:
can synchronize movements to a musical beat.

LENGTH	17¼–20 in	44–51 cm	DISTRIBUTION Native to north and
WINGSPAN	39 in	100 cm	eastern Australia and introduced
WEIGHT	1½–2 lb	700–950 g	to southwest; open woodland,
			parks, backyards, and suburbia.

TIME & DATE

LOCATION

BEHAVIOR

FEMALE-MALE

WEATHER

OTHER

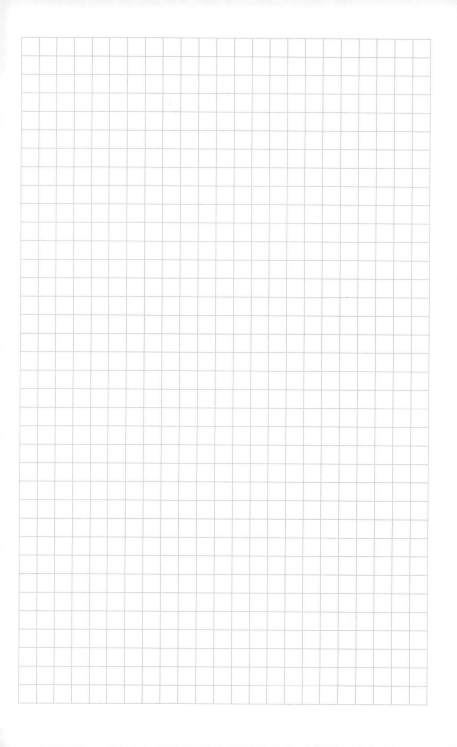

[46]

SUPERB FAIRYWREN

Malurus cyaneus

Tiny, with perky tail. Breeding male has electric blue markings; female browner. Hops about on ground in search of insects. Male and female form pairs, but each mates with multiple partners. Voted Australia's favorite bird in national poll.

LENGTH	5½ in	14 cm
WINGSPAN	8¾ in	±22 cm
WEIGHT	¼–½ oz	8–13 g

DISTRIBUTION Southeastern Australia, from Queensland to Tasmania; forests, heathland, and suburbia, common in Sydney and Melbourne.

TIME & DATE

LOCATION

BEHAVIOR

FEMALE-MALE

WEATHER

OTHER

[47]

SUPERB STARLING

Lamprotornis superbus

Iridescent blue/green upperparts contrast with red/orange belly.
Conspicuous white. Forages on ground for insects, fruits, and seeds,
typically below acacia trees. Bold and noisy, often hopping around
picnic sites.

LENGTH	7–7½ in	18–19 cm
WINGSPAN	±12 in	31 cm
WEIGHT	1¾–2¾ oz	52–77 g

DISTRIBUTION East Africa, from
Ethiopia to Tanzania; savannah and
open woodland, including in towns
and cultivated areas.

TIME & DATE

LOCATION

BEHAVIOR

FEMALE-MALE

WEATHER

OTHER

[48]

TURKEY VULTURE

Cathartes aura

Big and black with bare head. Scavenges on carrion, detecting food by smell. Soars and migrates on thermals, seldom flapping. More closely related to storks than to Old World vultures. Sometimes known, incorrectly, as "buzzard."

LENGTH	24–32 in	62–81 cm
WINGSPAN	63–72 in	160–183 cm
WEIGHT	1½–2 lb	45–60 g

DISTRIBUTION Americas, from Cape Horn to Canada; northern populations migrate south in winter; open habitats, urban areas.

TIME & DATE

LOCATION

BEHAVIOR

FEMALE-MALE

WEATHER

OTHER

WHITE-BREASTED KINGFISHER

Halcyon smyrnensis

Starling-sized, large bill and blue, white, and chestnut plumage.
Swoops down from branch or wire to capture frogs, reptiles, large
insects, and even other birds. Calls loudly during breeding season,
often from buildings.

LENGTH	10¼–11 in	26–28 cm
WINGSPAN	15¾–17 in	40–43 cm
WEIGHT	2½–4 oz	75–110 g

DISTRIBUTION Southern Asia, from Turkey to China; open country with wires and other perches, including in built-up areas.

TIME & DATE

LOCATION

BEHAVIOR

FEMALE-MALE

WEATHER

OTHER

[50]

WHITE-BREASTED NUTHATCH

Sitta carolinensis

Small and stocky, with strong bill and short tail. Climbs up and down tree trunks. Feeds on insects and seeds. Wedges acorns into crevice to break open (hence name). Smears insects around nest entrance to deter squirrels. Visits bird feeders.

LENGTH	5–5½ in	13–14 cm
WINGSPAN	8–10½ in	20–27 cm
WEIGHT	¾–1 oz	18–30 g

DISTRIBUTION North America, from southern Mexico to southern Canada; deciduous forest, using old trees for nest holes.

TIME & DATE

LOCATION

BEHAVIOR

FEMALE-MALE

WEATHER

OTHER

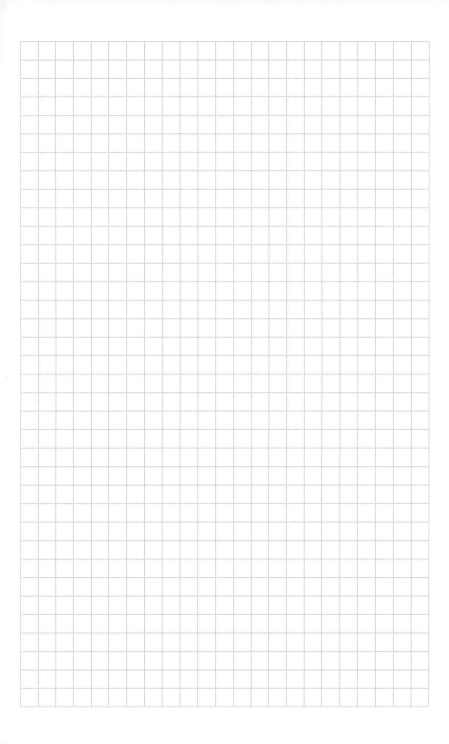

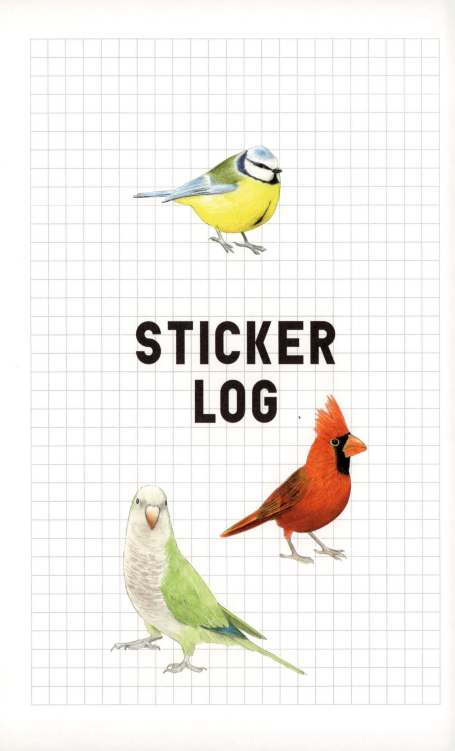

STICKER
LOG

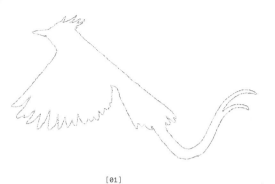

[01]
AFRICAN PARADISE FLYCATCHER
Terpsiphone viridis

[02]
AMERICAN GOLDFINCH
Spinus tristis

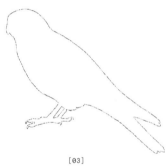

[03]
AMERICAN KESTREL
Falco sparverius

[04]
AMERICAN ROBIN
Turdus migratorius

[05]
BARN OWL
Tyto alba

[06]
BLUE JAY
Cyanocitta cristata

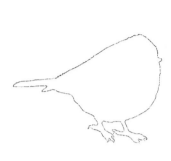

[07]
BLUE TIT
Cyanistes caeruleus

[08]
BOHEMIAN WAXWING
Bombycilla garrulus

[09]
BROWN PELICAN
Pelecanus occidentalis

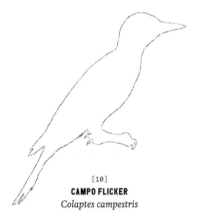

[10]
CAMPO FLICKER
Colaptes campestris

[11]
CANADA GOOSE
Branta canadensis

[12]
CAROLINA CHICKADEE
Poecile carolinensis

[13]
CAROLINA WREN
Thryothorus ludovicianus

[14]
CHINESE POND HERON
Ardeola bacchus

[15]
COMMON GRACKLE
Quiscalus quiscula

[16]
DARK-EYED JUNCO
Junco hyemalis

[17]
EASTERN BLUEBIRD
Sialia sialias

[18]
EUROPEAN BEE-EATER
Merops apiaster

[19]
EUROPEAN ROBIN
Erithacus rubecula

[20]
EUROPEAN STARLING
Sturnus vulgaris

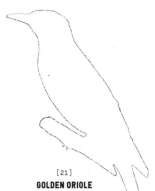

[21]
GOLDEN ORIOLE
Oriolus oriolus

[22]
GREAT BLUE HERON
Ardea herodias

[23]
GREAT HORNED OWL
Bubo virginianus

[24]
HAMERKOP
Scopus umbretta

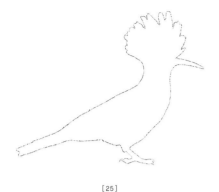

[25]
HOOPOE
Upupa epops

[26]
HOUSE SPARROW
Passer domesticus

[27]
LAUGHING KOOKABURRA
Dacelo novaeguineae

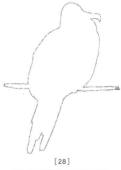

[28]
MAGNIFICENT FRIGATEBIRD
Fregata magnificens

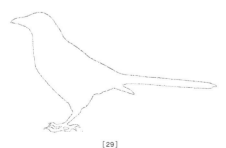

[29]
MAGPIE
Pica pica

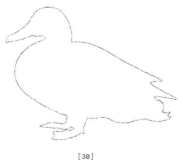

[30]
MALLARD
Anas platyrhynchos

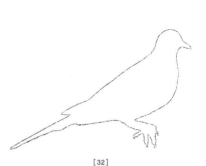

[31]
MONK PARAKEET
Myiopsitta monachus

[32]
MOURNING DOVE
Zenaida macroura

[33]
NORTHERN CARDINAL
Cardinalis cardinalis

[34]
NORTHERN MOCKINGBIRD
Mimus polyglottos

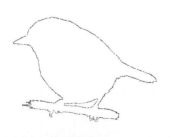

[35]
ORIENTAL WHITE-EYE
Zosterops palpebrosus

[36]
PEREGRINE FALCON
Falco peregrinus

[37]
PIED (WHITE) WAGTAIL
Motacilla alba

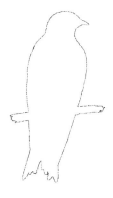

[38]
PURPLE MARTIN
Progne subis

[39]
RAINBOW LORIKEET
Trichoglossus moluccanus

[40]
RED-HEADED WOODPECKER
Melanerpes erythrocephalus

[41]
RED-WHISKERED BULBUL
Pycnonotus jocosus

[42]
RED-WINGED BLACKBIRD
Agelaius phoeniceus

[43]
RUBY-THROATED HUMMINGBIRD
Archilochus colubris

[44]
SERIN
Serinus serinus

[45]
SULPHUR-CRESTED COCKATOO
Cacatua galerita

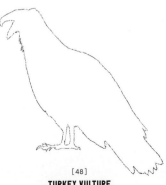

[46]
SUPERB FAIRYWREN
Malurus cyaneus

[47]
SUPERB STARLING
Lamprotornis superbus

[48]
TURKEY VULTURE
Cathartes aura

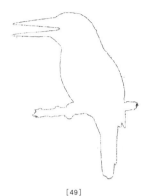

[49]
WHITE-BREASTED KINGFISHER
Halcyon smyrnensis

[50]
WHITE-BREASTED NUTHATCH
Sitta carolinensis